SPOKEN ARABIC – LEVEL3-

العاميّة الفَلَسْطينيّة / مُستوى تلاتة

بدّي أحْكي عَربي أحْسَن

Objectives:

1. The capacity to express one's will, intention, obligation, and possibility or desire to do something, using two consequent verbs, or certain words + a verb or the future structure.
2. Enhancing the vocabulary of verbs:

   Form I And form II.
3. Ability to talk about past or finished actions.
4. Ability to talk about repetitive/frequent actions using the present.
5. Giving instructions, demands or orders using imperative.
6. The ability to connect sentences and make them more coherent:

_ using the two major relative words: إلّي/ إنُّه

or words like before / as .....قبل ما/ بعد ما / زي ما

7. Capacity to talk about the space: vocabulary of bed room, kitchen… then in a larger sense necessary geographic terms.
8. Making better sentences by avoiding repetition: (using direct and indirect object pronouns).
9. Expressing surprise, admiration using (ما + comparative)

INDEX

الفَهْرَس

الوَزن الأوّل

مَجموعة1	المَعْنى	مَجموعة2	المَعْنى
راح		جاب	
كان		صار	
شاف		عاد	
قال		باع	
قام		غاب	
فات		زاح	
مات		عاش	
فاز		ضاع	
داق		طاب	
زار		قاس	
باس		طار	
		قام	
		فاق	

المَعْنى	مَجموعة4	المَعْنى	مَجموعة3
	كَتَب		نام
	دَرَس		خاف
	قَعَد		غار
	دَخَل		
	طَلَب		
	سَكَن		
	مَرَق		
	رَفَض		
	سَكَت		
	رَقَص		
	رَكَض		
	غَسَل		
	لَفَظ		
	طَبَخ		
	رَسَم		
	شَكَر		
	ضَرَب		
	سَرَق		
	هَرَب		
	رَبَط		
	أكَل*		

		*أخَذ	
مَجموعة5	المَعْنى	مَجموعة6	المَعْنى
عِمِل		نِسي	
قِدِر		صِحي	
عِرِف			
سِمِع			
فِهِم			
شِرِب			
لِعِب			
طِلِع			
نِزِل			
رِجِع			
وِصِل			
لِبِس			
شِلِح			
قِبِل			
حِضِر			
كِرِه			
غِلِط			
ضِحِك			
وِقِع			

سبِح			
زِعِل			
نِدِم			
مَجموعة7	المَعْنى	مَجموعة8	المَعْنى
فَتَح		عَزَم	
دَفَع		تَرَك	
قَرَأ		مَسَك	
سَأل		حَجَز	
شَرَح		كَذَب	
بَعَث		عَزَف	
نَجَح		كَسَر	
مَسَح		حَمَل	
رَفَع		خَبَز	
سَبَح			
قَطَع			
جَمَع			

المَعْنى	مَجموعة 10	المَعْنى	مَجموعة9
	حَبّ		حَكَى
	حَسّ		ضَوى
	مَلّ		طَفى
	رَنّ		*أجى
	حَلّ		مَشى
	عَدّ		شَكَى
	لَفّ		بَكى
	شَمّ		لَغى
	كَبّ		رَمى
	لَمّ		شَوى
			قَلى
			مَحى
			بَنى
			جَلى
			كَوى
			غَلى

المَعْنى	مَجموعة12	المَعْنى	مَجموعة11
	ظَلّ		رَدّ
			حَطّ
			ضَبّ
			صَفّ
			قَصّ
			دَقّ
			ضَبّ
			نَطّ

شو عْمِلت إمبارح

إمبارِح أنا قُمت مِن النّوم السيعة سَبعة الصُّبح. كُنِت كتير نَعسان عَشان اللّيلة الماضية نِمت مِتْأخّر. شْرِبت قَهْوِتي ولْبِست بْسُرعة عَشان كان عِندي إجتماع السيعة تَمنية ونُصّ. مَشيت لَمَحطة الباص مَع جاري وحَكينا مع بَعض بالعَرَبي بَس لِلأسَف ما فْهِمت كُل إشي. وهيك عْرِفت إنُّه **لازم أدْرُس** أكْتَر **عَشان بدّي أحكي عَرَبي أحْسن☺!!!!!**

وْصِلِت على الشُّغل عَالوَقت، وبَعد الإجتماع قَعَدت في مَكتبي وما شُفت وَلا مُوَظّف. كُنت كتير مَشغول وكَمان ما أكَلت وَقت الإسْتراحة.

السّيعة سِتّة المَسا دَخلِت عَلى البيت وكُنت كتيرجُعان وتَعبان.

أخَذت دوش وما طَبَخت ولا طَلَبت أكِل مِن بَرّا عَشان طْلعت مَع أصحابي ورُحنا على مَطْعم جديد. أكَلنا مَشاوي وشْربنا أرْجيلة ورْجعت على البيت السيعة عَشَرة، قَرأت شْوَي وبعدين نِمت.

أ- أُكتب/ي النَص مَع *هو*.

ب- قول/ي النَّص بالمُضارِع.

مَجموعة 1

راح (عَلى/ لَ/ عِند) كان (في) قام فات (عَلى/ لَ)
مات (مِن/ عَلى) قال (لَ) باس ساق
زار داق شاف فاز

	ماضي	مُضارِع	لازِم+
أنا	رُحت	بَروح	أروح
إحنا	رُحنا	منـ / بِنروح	نْروح
إنتَ	رُحت	بِتروح	تْروح
إنتِ	رُحتي	بِتروحي	تْروحي
إنتوا	رُحتوا	بِتروحوا	تْروحوا
هو	راح	بيروح	يروح
هي	راحَت	بِتروح	تْروح
هم	راحوا	بيروحوا	يْروحوا

سَمير: بِدّك تْروح مَعي عَلى السينما؟

رامي: لا، كُنْت هُناك الأُسبوع الماضي وشُفت فِلِم وما كان كتير حِلو. بِشَكِل عام، ما بَروح كتير على السينما!! قول لَسامية، مُمكن بِدها تْروح مَعَك ☺

أمِر	نَفي الأمِر
روح	ما تروح!
روحي	ما تروحي!
روحوا	ما تروحوا!

بِدّي

فِعِل

لازِم + مُضارع بِدون بـ

مُمكِن (Sub)

ضَروري

مَثلاً: أنا مِستَعجِل، لازِم أروح هلّأ!

المُستقبل: راح/رح + مُضارع بدون بـ

الأُسبوع الجاي إحنا راح نزور عَكّا☺

إوْصِل الجُمَل:

1. فوتوا	_ هي كتير عَيّانة
2. ما تسوق بْسُرعة	_ كتير زاكيِة!
3. ياولاد بوسوا	_ أنا بَفْهَم عَرَبي مْنيح!
4. زوري سِتّك يا لينا	_ عَلى الصَّف يا طُلّاب
5. روح على السّينما	_ بُكرا فيه مَدرَسة.
6. ما تفوتي على النّوم مِتأخّر	_ وشوف الفِلِم الجديد.
7. دوقي هادي الشّورَبَة	_ أنا مِش مِستَعجِل!!!!
8. قول شو بِدَّك	_ أبوكُم قَبِل النّوم.

راح دَرَس حَكى

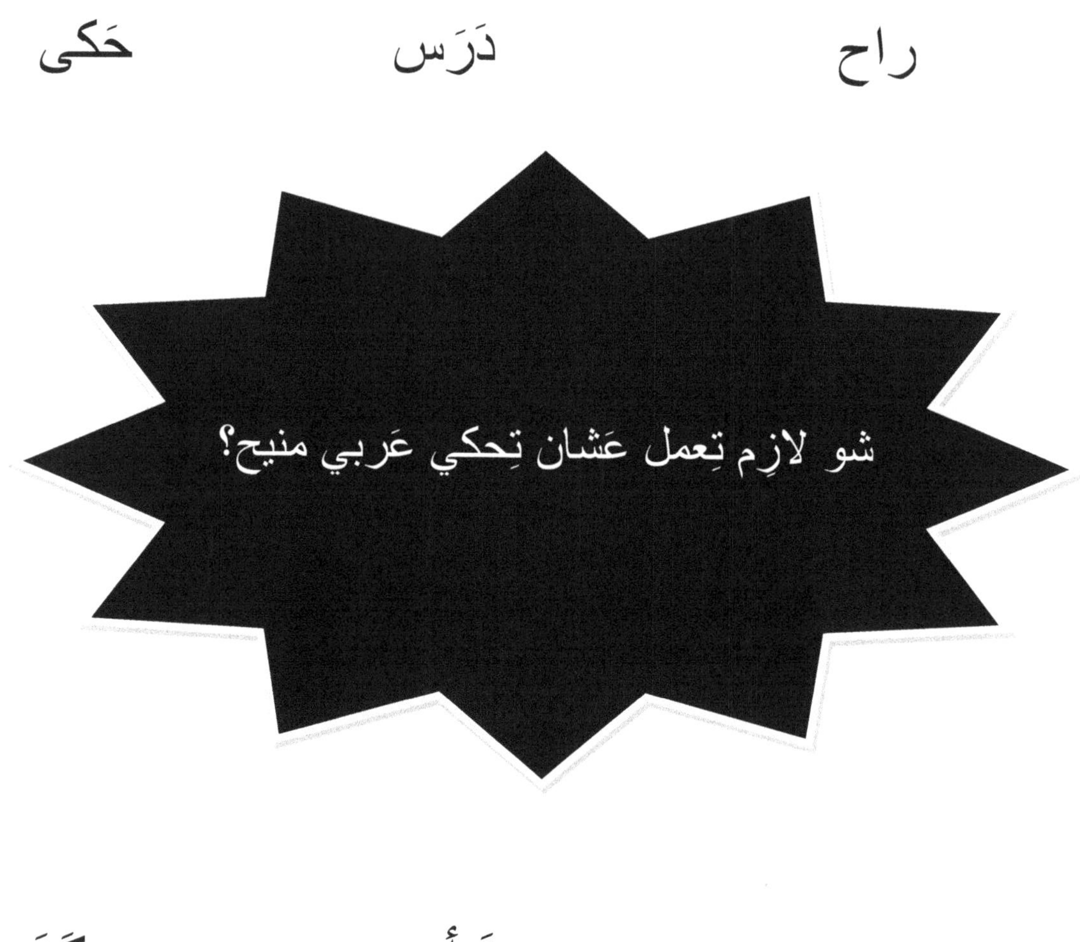

سِمِع قَرَأ كَتَب

أوّل إشي	تاني إشي	آخر إشي

مَجموعة 2

جاب غاب عَن طار

طاب صار

باع قاس (الأواعي) عاش # مات

ضاع زاح

	ماضي	مُضارِع	لازِم+
أنا	جِبت	بَجيب	أجيب
إحنا	جِبنا	بِنجيب	نْجيب
إنتَ	جِبت	بِتجيب	تجيب
إنتِ	جِبْتي	بِتجيبي	تجيبي
إنتوا	جِبتوا	بِتجيبوا	تجيبوا
هو	جاب	بيجيب	يجيب
هي	جابَت	بِتجيب	تجيب
هم	جابوا	بيجيبوا	يجيبوا

جيب الأغراض مِن السوق لو سَمحت!

الأمر نفي الأمر

جيب جيبي جيبوا ما تجيب! ما تجيبي! ما تجيبوا!

أُكتُب/ي جُمل مَع هَدول الكَلمات

1) غاب الدرس
2) جاب الأغراض
3) باع غالي
4) زار باريس شاف
5) قاس البلوزة الجديدة

مَجموعة 3

- حَبيبتي ما تخافي أنا هون معِك!!
- يلّا يا ولاد ناموا!!!!
- هو بيغار مِن أُختُه عَشان هي أشْطَر مِنّه!!

	ماضي	مُضارع	لازِم+
أنا	نِمِت	بَنام	أنام
إحنا	نِمنا	بِنّام	نّْام
إنتَ	نِمت	بِتنام	تنام
إنتِ	نِمتي	بِتنامي	تنامي
إنتوا	نِمتوا	بِتناموا	تناموا
هو	نام	بينام	ينام
هي	نامَت	بِتنام	تنام
هم	ناموا	بِيناموا	يناموا

نام نامي ناموا

ما تنام ما تنامي ما تناموا

مَجموعة 4

دَرَس	كَتَب	سَكَت	قَعَد	دَخَل	شَكَر	طَلَب	سَكَن
رَقَص	رَكَض	غَسَل	لَفَظ	طَبَخ	رَسَم	رَفَض	مَرَق

	ماضي	مُضارع	لازِم+
أنا	دَرَست	بَدْرُس	أدْرُس
إحنا	دَرَسنا	بِنُدْرُس	نُدْرُس
إنتَ	دَرَست	بِتُدْرُس	تُدْرُس
إنتِ	دَرَستي	بِتُدْرُسي	تُدْرُسي
إنتوا	دَرَستوا	بِتُدْرُسوا	تُدْرُسوا
هو	دَرَس	بيُدْرُس	يُدْرُس
هي	دَرْسَت	بِتُدْرُس	تُدْرُس
هم	دَرَسوا	بيُدْرسوا	يُدْرسوا

أُدْرُس　　أُدرُسي　　أُدْرُسوا

ما تُدْرُس !　　ما تُدْرُسي!　　ما تُدرُسوا!

- **هو كان كتير مَبسوط في الحَفلة ورَقص وما قَعَد!!!**
- **المعَلمة قالَت: يا طُلّاب لَو سَمَحتوا ألفُظوا منيح!!**
- **هَلّأ أنا ساكنة في القُدس بَس السّنة الماضية سَكَنت في حيفا**
- **أنا بَركُض مَرتين في الأُسبوع.**

- جاوِب عَلى الأسئلة:

1. أي سيعة لازِم تقوم/ي مِن النّوم كُل يوم وأي سيعة بِتنام/ي؟
2. شو طَبَخت/ي إمبارح؟
3. الطُّلّاب كَتبوا الوَظيفة؟
4. بِدّك تُقعُد/ي في البيت في آخِر الأُسبوع؟
5. مِن شو بِتخاف/ي؟
6. أكَم مَرّة بِتُركُض في الأُسبوع؟
7. بِتحبّ/ي تُرْسُم/ي؟
8. إنتَ غَسَلت السيّارة؟
9. في الحَفلة إنتَ دايماً بتُرقُص؟
10. مِن وين بِتجيب/ي الخُضْرة والفَواكِه؟

11. شو بتاكُل/ي الصُّبُح؟

12. بِدّك تاخُذ الباص ولّا السيّارة اليوم؟

أكَل*

	ماضي	مُضارع	لازِم+
أنا	أكَلت	باكُل	آكُل
إحنا	أكَلْنا	بناكُل/بنوكُل	ناكُل
إنتَ	أكَلت	بتاكُل/بتوكُل	تاكُل
إنتِ	أكَلتي	بتاكلي/بتوكلي	تاكلي
إنتوا	أكَلتوا	بتاكلوا/بتوكلوا	تاكلوا
هو	أكَل	بياكُل/بيوكُل	ياكُل
هي	أكْلَت	بتاكُل/بتوكُل	تاكُل
هم	أكَلوا	بياكلوا/بيوكلوا	ياكلوا

كُل كُلي كُلوا

ما تاكُل! ما تاكلي! ما تاكلوا!

_ راح تاكُل مَعنا؟

_ لأ شكراً، أنا شَبعان، قبل شْوَي أكَلت!

- أخَذ

	ماضي	مُضارع	لازِم+
أنا			
إحنا			
إنتَ			
إنتِ			
إنتوا			
هو			
هي			
هم			

جاوِب/ي على الأسئلة و أُكتب/ي كَمان تلاتة:

1. إيمتى بتشوف أصْحابك؟
2. بتِحِب تزور روما؟
3. إنتَ لازِم تجيب الولاد مِن المَدرسة اليوم؟

4. هم باعوا سيّارتهم؟
5. إنتوا مُمكِن تُطلبوا الأكِل مِن بَرّا اليوم؟
6. هو ساق سيّارتُه اليوم ولا أخذ الباص؟
7. هم داقوا الكنافِة؟
8. هي بتُلفُظ الكَلمات بالعَربي صَح؟
9. هو بِدُّه يبيع بيته السّنة الجاية؟
10. إنتوا بِدكُم تُشكروا أبوكُم ؟

كمّل الجدول

الفعل	ماضي أنا	مضارع أنا	أمِر إنتَ	نفي الأمِر إنتَ
كان				
جاب				
نام				
كَتَب				
أكَل				

مَجموعة5

شِرِب لِعِب ضِحِك(على)

طِلِع(على/ مَن) نِزِل(مِن عَن) حِضِر

رِجِع سِمِع (الأخبار/ الأغاني.....)

عِمِل (سَلَطة / يوغا / الوَظيفة/ الإمتحان/جيم)

فِهِم لِبِس(الأواعي/ الطقيّة/ النظّارة)

عِرِف قِدِر زِعِل (مِن)

كِرِه غِلِط

_ يا طُلّاب، عمِلتوا الوَظيفة؟

_ أيوا عْمِلناها، بَس ما فْهِمنا كُلّ التمرين.

_ يا ولاد لازِم تِشرَبوا الحَليب!

_ إحنا شْرِبناه.

عِمِل

	ماضي	مُضارع	لازِم+
أنا	عْمِلت	بَعمَل	أعْمَل
إحنا	عْمِلنا	بْنِعمَل	نِعمَل
أنتَ	عْمِلت	بْتعمَل	تِعمَل
إنتِ	عْمِلتي	بْتعمَلي	تِعمَلي
إنتوا	عْمِلتوا	بْتعمَلوا	تِعمَلوا
هو	عِمِل	بْيعمَل	يِعمَل
هي	عِمْلت	بْتعمَل	تِعمَل
هم	عِمْلوا	بْيعمَلوا	يِعمَلوا

الأمر:

إعْمَل ما تِعمَل!

إعْمَلي ما تِعمَلي!

إعْمَلوا ما تِعمَلوا !

أُكتب الأفعال بالشّكَل المُناسِب:

رامي: في نهاية الأُسبوع أنا وصحابي راح_______ على حيفا.(طِلِع)

لينا: بِدكُم______(ساق) ولا راح _______ (أخذ) القِطار

؟

رامي: راح ______ (راح) بالسيّارة.

لينا: بِدكُم ______ (نام) هُناك؟

رامي: أيوا، راح ________ (قَعَد) بأوتيل جَنب البَحَر ومُمكن______ (رِجِع) الأحد الظُّهر أو المَسا. بِدِّك تيجي مَعنا؟

أجى# راح

لينا: لِلأسَف، عِندي إمتحان عربي ولازم_______ (دَرَس) وما بَقدر_______ (غاب) عن الشُّغل يوم الجُمعة.

أُكتُب النّص في الماضي:

في نهاية الأُسبوع رامي وأصحابه ....

كمّل بالأمر:

1. يا طُلّاب ______ (فات) على الصّف
و________(عِمِل) الإمتحان لو سَمحتوا!!
2. ما ________ (طَبَخ) اليوم يا فادي بِدنا نروح على المَطعم.
3. يا ولاد، لمّا تُدخلوا على المَكتبة______ (سَكَت)
لَوْ سَمَحتوا و ______ (سِمِع) الموظّفة شو بِتقول.
4. يا سامي، ما ________ (ضِحِك) لمّا أُختَك الصغيرة بتُلفظ الحُروف غَلَط.
5. ______ (نام) بكّيرو ______(قام) بكّير و
_____(شاف) الصّحة كيف بِتصير!!!!(إنتَ)

☺

6.لو سمحت يا سامي، ما ________ (رِجِع) متأخّر اليوم من الشّغل، و ______ خُبز من المَخبز.(جاب)

7.يلّا يا مُنى _________(قاس) هادي البلوزة الجديدة و _____ مَعْها البنطلون الأسود(لِبِس).

مَجموعة 6

ما تِنسوا الوظيفة يا طُلّاب!

_ ما بعرف وين تلفوني!!!
_ مُمكِن نسيتُه بالبيت!

	ماضي	مُضارِع	لازم+	أمِر
أنا	نْسيت	بَنسى	أنسى	
إحنا	نْسينا	بْنِنسى	نِنسى	
إنتَ	نْسيت	بْتِنسى	تِنسى	**إنْسى**
إنتِ	نْسيتي	بْتنسي	تِنسي	**إنْسي**
إنتوا	نْسيتوا	بْتِنسوا	تِنسوا	**إنْسوا**
هو	نِسي	بْيِنسى	يِنسى	
هي	نِسْيَت	بْتِنسى	تِنسى	
هم	نِسْيوا	بْيِنسوا	يِنسوا	

_ أنا دايماً بَنسى تَلفوني بالبيت وإنتَ شو دايماً بْتنسى/بتنسي؟

_ إمبارِح نسيت تِطفي البيت لما رُحِت على الشُّغل؟

أنا لازِم أكتُب الكَلِمات الجديدة عَشان ما __________ ها!

عادةً شو بتِنسى؟ أي سيعة كُلّ يوم بتِصحى؟

شو الأفعال الممُكنة مع هَدول الكلمات؟؟

البَلْدة القديمة عيّان

الدَّرس

الحُروف والكَلِمات

رُز وجاج السيّارة

الجاكيت مُفتاح البيت

بكّير الحَفْلة

الإجتماع الأغاني

مَجموعة 7

فَتَح دَفَع 1. (حقّ/ الفاتورة=الحساب) 2. زاح
شَرَح
سَأل قَرَأ مَسَح جَمَع
رَفَع بَعَث

ماضي	مُضارع	لازم +	أمِر
فَتَحت	بَفْتَح	أفْتَح	
فَتَحْنا	بْنِفْتَح	نِفْتَح	
فَتَحت	بْتِفْتَح	تِفْتَح	**إفْتَح**
فَتَحْتي	بْتِفْتَحي	تِفْتحي	**إفْتَحي**
فَتَحْتوا	بْتِفتَحوا	تِفْتحوا	**إفْتَحوا**
فَتَح	بْيفتَح	يِفْتح	
فَتْحَت	بِتفْتَح	تِفْتح	
فَتَحوا	بْيِفْتَحوا	يِفتَحوا	

ما تِفتَح ! **ما تِفتحي!** **ما تِفتحوا!**

كمّل: _أنا كَتَبِت الإيميل بَس لِسّا ما ______ (بَعَث).

_ إنتَ دَفَعِت فاتورة المَي؟ أيوا_______.

_ ما ______ الشُّبّاك لو سَمَحتي برّا كتير بَرد.

أُكتب/ي تلات أسئلة وتلات أجوبة مَع أفعال مِن مَجموعة (فَتَح)

____

____

____

____

____

____

كَمّل بالأمر مع الفعِل المُناسب من مَجموعة **فَتَح :**

1. يا طُلّاب ______ الأسئلة وإذا مش فاهمين ________!
2. المُدير للسكرتيرة: لو سمحتي ______ بَرنامج الدورة للطّلاب!

3. لو سَمَحت ________ فاتورة المَي بعد الشغل!

مَجموعة8

كَسَر	تَرَك	مَسَك
عَزَم	حَجَز (تذكرة/ تاكسي/ غُرفِة)	
	عَزَف	

حَجَز

	ماضي	مُضارع	SUB
أنا	حَجَزت	بحْجِز	أحْجِز
إحنا	حَجَزْنا	بنحْجِز	نِحْجِز
إنتَ	حَجَزت	بتحْجِز	تِحْجِز
إنتِ	حَجَزتي	بتِحْجِزي	تِحْجِزي
إنتوا	حَجَزتوا	بتِحْجِزوا	تِحْجِزوا
هو	حَجَز	بيِحْجِز	يِحْجِز
هي	حَجْزَت	بتِحْجِز	تِحْجِز
هم	حَجَزوا	بيحْجِزوا	يِحْجِزوا

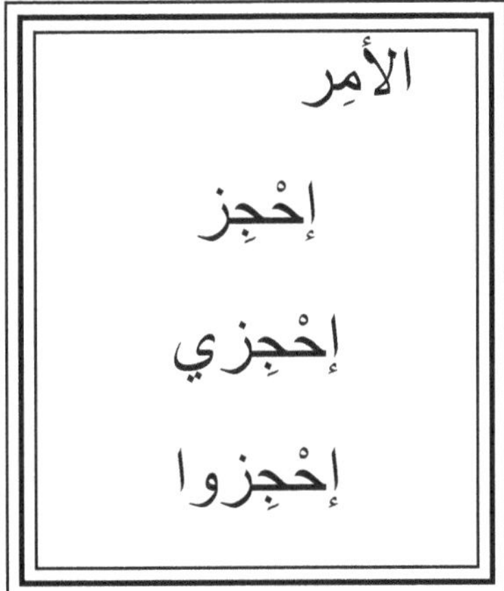

نفي الأمِر

ما تِحْجِز!

ما تِحْجِزي!

ما تِحْجِزوا

1.لو سمحت بدّي **أحْجِز** طاولة لخَمس أشخاص.

2. بُكرا عيد ميلادي وبِدّي **أعْزِمكم** عندي.

3. شفتوا تلفوني؟ إنتِ **تَركتيه** على الطاولة.

4. لو سمحت **إحْمِل** معي الخزانة الجديدة.

5. يا ولاد ما تِرموا الطابة على الشُّباك مُمكن **تِكْسِروه!!!**

6. حَبيبي **إمْسِك** إيد أُختك في الشارع وشوفوا السيّارات منيح!

7. سَمير **بْيعزِف** پيانو كتير منيح!!!

8. الوَلد جاب علامة مِش منيحة بَس هو **كَذَب** و قال إنّه نَجَح!!!!

9. لمّا رُحت على السوق كان فيه كتير ناس، جُزداني ضاع ولّا **سَرَقوه!**

أُكتبوا حوارات مَع:

أنا وصاحِب المَطْعَم

/السيعة 8 المَسا/ طاولة / شَخص/ حَجَز/ الأرْبَعا

الإم وإبِنها

مَشى/ لمّا/ مَسَك/ في الشارع/ دير بالَك/ السيّارات/ شاف/ أُختك/ إيد

سمير وميرا

في المُسابَقة / عَزَف/ الأُسبوع الجاي/ حِضِر/ بدّي/ على البيانو

سَلمى وزُمَلاءِ ها في الشُّغُل

تِسعة الشّهِر/عَزَم / عيد ميلاد/ يوم الخَميس/ عندي/ أجى/
مع العيلة

مجموعة9

1. حَكى
2. ضَوى
3. طَفى
4. كَوى
5. جَلى
6. شَوى
7. قَلى
8. رَمى
9. مَشى
10. غَلى
11. مَحى
12. بَكى
13. بَنى
14. شَكى
15. أجى*
16. لَغى

شو الفِعل المُناسِب:

الصحون والكاسات   **الطّابِة**   **للشّغُل**

لأنُّه زعَلان   **الفلافِل والبطاطا**   **المَي للشّاي**

عَرَبي وإنجليزي   **الضَو والكمبيوتر**   **الأواعي**

الشَمِع والضَو   **اللوح /الغلط**   **الإجتماع**

اللّحمة   **مِن الصّوت/ مِن الجيران**   **على الدرس**

	ماضي	مُضارع	لازم+	أمر
أنا	حَكيت	بَحكي		
إحنا	حَكينا	بنِحكي		
إنتَ	حَكيت	بتِحكي		إحْكي
إنتِ	حَكيتي	بتِحكي		إحْكي
إنتوا	حَكيتوا	بتِحكوا		إحْكوا
هو	حَكى	بيِحكي		
هي	حَكت	بتِحكي		
هم	حَكوا	بيِحكوا		

أجى

	ماضي	مُضارع	لازم+	أمر
أنا	(ا)جيت	باجي	آجي	
إحنا	(ا)جينا	بنيجي	نيجي	
إنتَ	(ا)جيت	بتيجي	تيجي	تَعال
إنتِ	(ا)جيتي	بتيجي	تيجي	تَعالي
إنتوا	(ا)جيتوا	بتيجوا	تيجوا	تَعالوا
هو	*أجى	بيجي	يجي	
هي	*أجَت	بتيجي	تيجي	
هم	*أجوا	بيجوا	يجوا	

المُدير: يا مُوظَّفين، الرِحلة بُكرا بَكّير والباص راح يكون هون السّيعة سَبعة الصّبُح، ما تيجوا مِتأخِّر!!!!!

ما تيجي! **ما تيجي!** **ما تيجوا!**

أكتُب/ي جُمل بالأمِر أو نفي الأمِر:

1. طَلَب بيتزا عَزَم

2. مَسَح الأرْض جَلى

3. جاب الأغراض دَفَع

4. نِسي المُفتاح طَفى

5. تَرَك السَيّارة مَشى

6. شَوى اللّحْمة قَلى

7. أخَذ الباص راح

8. كَذَب سَرَق

جاوب عَلى الاسئلة مَع زَميلك/ زميلتك:

1.أكم لُغة بْتعرَف تِحكي؟
2. مِن شو دايماً الطُلاب بيشكوا؟
3. بِتْحبّ تِكوي؟ مين بيكوي أواعيك؟
4. جَليت بعد الأكل؟
5. بتفضّل تِشوي ولا تِقْلي البطاطا؟
6. وين بِتحبّ تمشي؟
7. كُل يوم بْتضوي الكُمبيوتر؟

كمّل مع هَدول الأفعال بالماضي أو الأمر:

رَقَص/ سِمِع / نام / سَأل/ كان2 / أجى/ صار/ قِدر/ شَكى/ فات / رِجِع /طَفى

أنا وَلا مَرّة_______ مِن جيراني! بَس ليلة إمبارح ما _____
أنام طول اللّيل عَشان_____عِندهُم حَفلة. أوّل إشي
لمّا________ الأغاني _______ مَبسوطة!
بَس لمّا______ وَقت النّوم رُحت عِنْدهم و______ : لإيمتى
الحَفلة؟؟

قالوا:تْفَضّلي ______ على البيت. يَلّا ________ و _________ مَعنا في الحفلة!!!!

بَس أنا كُنت نَعْسانِة : _____ على بيتي_______ الضّو بس ما ☹ _____ مِن الصّوت!!!!

كمّل بالمُضارِع او SUB والضمير اذا لازِم:

أنا وصاحبي كتير مُخْتَلفين

لمّا أنا ________ (مَشى) هو بيحبّ __________ (رَكَض).
أنا _________ (شَوى) اللّحمة والجاج وهو بيفضّل _________ (قَلى).
أنا بَكره _________ (كَوى) القُمصان وهو دايماً__________ (كَوى).
بعد الشُّغل أنا دايماً_______(رَقَص) و_________مَبسوطة (كان) وهو __________ (شَكى) من الشّغُل.
أنا __________ كُل البيت(ضَوى) وهو بِيحِبّ العِتمة و________(طَفى).
أنا __________ (طَبَخ) تَقريباً كل يوم بَس هو بيحِبّ_________ أكل من بَرّا.(طَلَب)
أنا _________ كتير(حَكى) وهوبيفضّل _________ و _________

(سَكَت/سِمِع)

أنا ________ بكّير(نام) و________ بكّير(قام) وهو ________ (فات) ينام متأخرّ و ________ بَكّير.(صِحي) و مَع هيك إحنا دايماً ________ (عِمِل) كُل شي مَع بَعض!!!!!!!

جاوب على الأسئلة مع الضَمير:

1. إنتَ أخَذت السّيارة؟ ________________
2. أي سيعة راح تْشوف صْحابَك اليوم؟ ________________
3. السكرتيرة بعثَت الإيميل للمُدير؟ ________________
4. طَفيت ضْواو البيت لمّا طْلِعت؟ ________________
5. الولاد أكَلوا البيتزا ؟ ________________
6. إنتوا عْملتوا الوَظيفة؟ ________________
7. راح تِشْووا اللّحمة في الحَفلة؟ ________________
8. أيْ سيعة لازم تْجيب الكُتب مِن المَكتبة؟ ________________

1. كمّل مع الفِعل المناسب بالأمِر:

مَشى/ سِمِع/ مَحى/ زِعِل/ لِبس / حَكى/ خاف/ ضَرَب/ نِسي/ شكى/ ضوى/

1. يا ولاد ________ الجاكيتات لأنُّه بَرا بَرد.

2. ________ مشاكِل الشُّغل لمّا تفوت على البيت!!

3. ________ مع المُدير، هو سَأل وين كنتِ!

4. ________ المكيّف لو سَمَحت، كتير شوب.

5. ________ للشُّغل أحْسن فيه كتير أزمِة هاي السيعة!

6. ما ________ من الكَلب الكبير لأنُّه لَطيف!!

7. ما ________ و ما ________ كُل الوقت، كل مُشكلة إلها حَل!!!

8. ________ يا ولاد شو بِتقول الماما و ما ________ بَعض!

مَجموعة 10

حَسّ إنُّه **حَسّ مَع**

_ أنا **حَسّيت** إنُّه المُدير زَعْلان اليوم!

_ زميلي **بِحِسّ** مَعي لَمّا بيكون عِندي كتير شُغُل.

عَدّ

هو عَدّ المَصاري لمّا دَخَل على البنك!

مَلّ من **رَنّ لَـ /على** **حَلّ الوظيفة/ المُشْكلة**

حَبّ # كِرِه **كَبّ الزبالِة** **شَمّ الرّيحة**

لَفّ على اليمين/ الشْمال / لَفّة

سَبّ على = غِلِط على

حَسّ

	ماضي	مُضارِع	لازم+	أمِر
أنا	حَسّيت	بَحِسّ	أحِسّ	
إحنا	حَسّينا	بِنْحِسّ	نْحِسّ	
أنتَ	حَسّيت	بِتْحِسّ	تْحِسّ	حِسّ
إنتِ	حَسّيتي	بِتْحِسّي	تْحِسّي	حِسّي
إنتوا	حَسّيتوا	بِتحِسّوا	تْحِسّوا	حِسّوا
هو	حَسّ	بيحِسّ	يْحِسّ	
هي	حَسّت	بِتحِسّ	تْحِسّ	
هم	حَسّوا	بيحِسّوا	يْحِسّوا	

ما تسِبّ   ما تسِبّي   ما تسِبّوا!

مَجموعة 11

حَطّ

	ماضي	مُضارِع	لازم+	أمِر
أنا	حَطّيت	بَحُطّ	أحُطّ	
إحنا	حَطّينا	بِنْحُطّ	نْحُطّ	
أنتَ	حَطّيت	بِتْحُطّ	تْحُطّ	حُطّ
إنتِ	حَطّيتي	بِتْحُطّي	تْحُطّي	حُطّي
إنتوا	حَطّيتوا	بِتحُطّوا	تْحُطّوا	حُطّوا
هو	حَطّ	بيحُطّ	يْحُطّ	
هي	حَطّت	بِتحُطّ	تْحُطّ	
هم	حَطّوا	بيحُطّوا	يْحُطّوا	

ما تُحطّ ! ما تحُطّي! ما تحُطّوا!

- يا فادي، وين ______ السيّارة؟ مَمنوع ______ هُناك؟
- ولاد أخوي كتير شاطرين بيسمعوا الكلمة ودايماً_______.
- قَبِل العُرُس هي ______ شَعرها وهيك حلو عَليها!
- البيت كتير فَوضى أنا لازِم ________!

ضَبّ	قَصّ	صَفّ	ردّ

شو الأفْعال المُناسبة مَع هَدول الكَلمات؟

الفاتورة **الأرض** **الأصحاب**

غُرفة في الأوتيل **الضّو**

البلوزة الجديدة **السَيّارة**

الوَردة الوظيفة المُفتاح

اللّوح الصّحون و الكاسات الزّبالة

شَعَرها لَلعَشرة التّلفون

السَّمَك والخُضرا دورة عَربي عَلى الباب

مَجموعة 12

ظَلّ

1. هم ظَلّوا في البيت في نِهاية الأُسْبوع = قَعَدوا

2. قَدّيش راح تْظَلّ في القُدس؟ = راح تكون في...

3. هو بيظلّ يِحكي طول الوَقت!!! ما سَكَت!!

	ماضي	مُضارِع	لازم+	أمِر
أنا	ظَلّيت	بَظَلّ	أظَلّ	
إحنا	ظَلّينا	بِنظَلّ	نْظَلّ	
أنتَ	ظَلّيت	بِتظَلّ	تْظَلّ	ظَلّ
إنتِ	ظَلّيتي	بِتظَلّي	تْظَلّي	ظَلّي
إنتوا	ظَلّيتوا	بتظَلّوا	تْظَلّوا	ظَلّوا
هو	ظَلّ	بيظَلّ	يْظَلّ	
هي	ظَلّت	بتظَلّ	تْظَلّ	
هم	ظَلّوا	بيظلّوا	يْظلّوا	

ما تظلّ تِشكي! **ما تْظَلّي زعلانة!**

ما تظلّوا في البيت تَعالوا معناّ

جاوِب/ي على الأسئلة مَع الضَمير إذا مُمكن:

1. مِن شو إنتَ بِتمِلّ؟
2. بِتْحِبّ فَصل الصّيف وِلّا الشِّتا؟
3. بِتْحِسّ مع أصْحابِك لمّا بيكونوا زَعْلانين؟
4. بتفضّل تظَلّ في البيت وِلّا تِطلع في نِهاية الأُسبوع؟
5. الولاد ضبّوا غُرْفِتهم؟
6. بِتْشمّ الأكل قَبل ما تدوقُه؟
7. وين حطّيت مُفتاح البيت؟
8. رَدّيت على الإيميل إلّي بَعثُه المُدير؟

9. وين بِتصُفّ سيّارتك لمّا بتيجي على دَرْس العَربِي؟

10. بِتحِبّ تْلِفّ في البَلدة القَديمة؟

11. دَلّيت الطُلّاب كيف يروحوا على المَكتبة؟

حَفلة عيد ميلاد إبني وراس السّنة

إختار/ي الجواب الصحيح:

سَلمى و صاحباتها:

سَلمى: يا صبايا، بدي ________(أحْجِزكُم/ أعْزِمكُم) على حفلة في واحد وتلاتين الشهر.

صاحباتها: يَعني حفلة راس السّنة؟

سَلمى: آه، بس كمان ________ (بيكون/ بيصير) عيد ميلاد إبني.

صاحباتها: عَن جدّ، قدّيش__________ (صار/ راح يصير) عمرُه؟

سَلمى: ______ (عشرة سنة/ عَشر سنين).

صاحباتها: شو ممكن __________ (ناخدُه/ نجيبلُه)؟

سَلمى: لو سَمحتوا ما ________ (جابوا/ تجيبولُه) ألعاب، عندُه ______ (خمسة طابات/ خَمِس طابات) و

__________ (سِتّعْشر پُزِل / سِتّعش پُزِلات).

وطبعاً هو كُل الوقت ________ (لازِم يِلعَب/ بيظَلّ يِلعَب) على تلفونُه.

لينا: أنا _____ (بَضُبّ / بحِسّ) _____ (أنُّه/ إلّي) أحسن هديّة لهادا العُمُر هي الكُتُب.

سَلمى: _______ (مَعِك حَقّ/ وَلَو) هادي ______ (فِكْرة/ رِحلة) مُمتازة!!!

ليلى: بدِّك_______ (مُساعدة/ مُشكلة) للحفلة؟

سَلمى: _______ (بَشكُركُم/ شَكَرتُهم) كتير، مين ______ (بْتِقدر / قِدرت)_________ (تُطْبُخ/ تِعْمَل) سَلطة عَربيّة؟

ليلى: أنا كتير ______ (حِبّ/ بَحِبّ) ________ (أعملُه/ أعْمَلها). بس أكم من حبّة بندورة وخيار لازِم_______ (أدُقّ/ أحُطّ/ أجيب) _____ (عليها/فيها)؟

سَلمى: لَو سَمَحتي، _______ (ما تحُطّي فيها/ حُطّي فيها) ________ (تلاتَة حبّة بَندورة/ تلات حَبّات بَندورة)

و________ (أربَع خيارات/ أربَع خيار) و ________

(ما تِصحي/ ما تِنسي) البَقدونس والبَصَل!!!

ليلى: هيك بِكَفّي، أكم من ______ (شَخص/ ناس/ أشْخاص)

________ (راح يجوا/ راح يجي/ راح يفوتوا) على الحَفلة؟

سَلمى: راح ______ (يصير / يكون/ تكون)________

(منها/ فيها/ عليها) تقريباً__________(خَمسة وعشرين

أشخاص/ عِشرين شخص/ خمِس وعِشرين شَخَص).

سميرة: أنا _________ (شايفِة/ مسافرِة/ ظايلة) على

إيطاليا عَشان هيك لِلأسف__________(ما راح آجي/ ما

بروح/ ما إجيت). بَس ________ (راح آخدُه/ راح أجيبلُه)

هديّة حِلوة من هُناك.

لينا : قدّيش ___________(راح تقعدوا/ راح تظَلّي/ ظَلّيتي)

هُناك؟

سَميرة: __________ (تنين أُسبوع/ أُسبوعتين/ أُسبوعين).

سَلمى: أهلاً وسهلاً __________ (مِنكم/ مَعكُم/ فيكُم).

☺☺☺

إلّي/ إنُّه

*شفتوا الطّالِب الجديد **إلّي** أجى اليوم؟

*المعلمة قالت **إنُّه** الإمتحان طويل!!!

إسِم+ إلّي

فِعِل + إنُّه

- الولاد أكلوا السّلَطة إلّي كانت بالتّلاجة.
- السِكرتيرة فَكّرت إنُّه العُطلة بُكرا بَس المُدير قال إنّه لِسّا الأُسبوع الجاي!

أُكتب **إلّي** أو **إنُّه** وبعدين كَمّل هَدول الأسئلة:

شُفت المعلمة ____________________________________ ؟

قرأتي الكتاب ____________________________________ ؟

بِتحسّوا____________________________________ ؟

إنتَ فكّرت زيي ____________________________________ ؟

سمعت الأُغنية____________________________________ ؟

جبتلّي الأغراض____________________________________ ؟

ردّيت على الإيميل ____________________________________ ؟

مين قال____________________________________ ؟

رُحتوا على المَطعم____________________________________ ؟

عَن جَدّ المُدير خَبّر المُوظّفين____________________________________ ؟

إلّي فات مات!!

شو يعني هادا المثل☺؟؟؟

____

أُكتب جُمَل مَع إلّـي:

مثلاً:

المدرسة هي المكان إلّي الولاد بيدرسوا فيه.

1. المَطْعَم - طَلَب/ أكَل
2. المَعْهَد – دَرَس
3. المَطْبَخ - طَبَخ
4. المَلْعب - لِعِب
5. غُرفة النوم - نام/ لِبِس
6. المَطار – طِلِع/ نِزِل

غُرْفة النّوم

1.تَخت_ تخوت

2.مْخَدّة– مخدّات (فْراش= كُل إشي على التَّخت)

3.سِجّادة– سِجّاد

4.كومودينا–كومودينات

5.مْراية– مُري

6.خَزانة– خَزاين

7.ضَوْ– ضْواو

8.رَفّ–رْفوف

9 . جَرّار_ جَوارير

9.بُرْداي– بَرادي

المَطْبَخ

تلّاجة- تلّاجات فُرن– فران غاز – غازات

مَجلى– مَجالي حَنَفيّة– حَنفيّات

مَعْلقة– مَعالِق شوكة– شُوَك سِكّينة– سَكاكين

كاسة–كاسات فِنجان–فَناجين صَحِن–صحون

صونية/ صينية– صواني طَنْجرة_ طَناجِر

إبريق قلّاية

*إحكي عَن واحد مِن أغراض المَطبخ أوغُرفة النّوم، وزُمَلاءك لازِم يِعرفوا شو هو؟

مثلاً: هادا إشي بِنحُطّه على الشَّبابيك عَشان نور الشّمس ما يُدخل والجيران ما يشوفونا ☺ شو هادا؟ ....

كيف ما / بَدل ما / زَي ما / إيمتى ما/ قَد ما / وين ما/بِدون ما

+ فِعِل

بُكرا أنا فاضية تَعال ________ تِقدر !!

تفضّلي أُقعدي ________ تحبّي!!!

أُمرُق على المَكتب ________ يخلَص الدَرس.

إقرأ كْتاب ________ تِحْضَر تَلفزيون كل الوقت.

فيه كتير سَلَطة، كُلوا ________ ما بِدكُم.

ما أحْلى هالفُستان!!!

ما أشْطَر هالطُّلاب!!!! ما + Comparative= كتير

...... ما ________ هادا الدُّكان.(غالي) ما ________ هالمطعم(زاكي).

الوزن التاني

مجموعة1

أنا **فَكَّرِت** إنُّه الإمْتحان بُكرا!

تلفوني ضاع. أنا **دَوَّرت** عليه كُلّ اليوم!

هو بيحِبّ العَرَبي و**سَجّل** في پولِس عشان يُدرس هُناك.

دَرْس العَرَبي **بيبَلِّش** السّيعة ستّة ونُص.

ضُبّ الأواعي وأنا **بَكَمِّل** أضُب البيت.

المَعنى	الفِعل
	فَكّر
	دَوّر/فَتّش
	صَلّح
	خَبّر
	رَكّز
	بَلّش
	كَمّل
	خَلّص
	رَوّح
	غَيّر
	بَدّل
	صَوّر
	سَجّل
	رَتّب

	نَظّف# وَسّخ
	ذَكّر
	فَضّل
	سَكّر
	رَجّع
	قَرّر
	عَلّم
	وَدّع
	حَضّر
	جَرّب
	قَطّع
	قَشّر

أمِر	لازم +	مُضارع	ماضي
	أفْكِّر	بَفَكِّر	فَكّرت

فَكَّرنا	بِنْفَكِّر	نْفَكِّر	
فَكَّرت	بِتْفَكِّر	تْفَكِّر	فَكِّر
فَكَّرتي	بِتْفَكْري	تْفَكْري	فَكْري
فَكَّرتَوا	بِتْفَكْروا	تْفَكْروا	فَكْروا
فَكَّر	بْيفَكِّر	يْفَكِّر	
فَكَّرت	بِتفَكِّر	تْفَكِّر	
فَكَّروا	بْيفَكْروا	يْفَكْروا	

ما تْفَكِّر كتير: كُل مُشْكلة وإِلها حَلّ!!

ما تفَكْري! **ما تفَكْروا!**

جاوِب/ي مَع الضَّمير إذا لازِم:

1. شو قَرّرت على السّنة الجديدة؟
2. هم فَكّروا كيف يحِلّوا المُشكِلة؟
3. بدّك تسجّل في مُستوى أربعة؟
4. تَلفوني خربان، وين مُمْكن أصَلحُه؟

5. إيمتى بَلّشت دورة العربي وإيمتى راح تخلّص؟
6. لسّا هم بيدَوْروا على شُغُل؟
7. بْتِقدر تِسمَع أغاني وتركّز في الشّغل؟
8. بعد العربي راح تْجرّب تُدْرُس لُغة جديدة؟
9. لمّا بِتروح مَكان جديد بِتظَلّ تْصوّر؟
10. نَظّفت البيت ورَتّبت غُرفتك؟

_المَسيحيّين **بِيصَلّوا** في الكنيسة يوم الأحَد

والمُسلمين **بيصَلّوا** في المَسجد يوم الجُمعة

واليَهود **بيصَلّوا** في الكنيس يوم السّبت.

- أنا **سَوّيت** كَعكة شوكلاطة.

- أنا **سَوّيت** الوَظيفة.

- شو **بِتْسَوّي**؟

_ فيروز **غنّت** كتير في لُبنان وفي كتير بُلدان عَرَبيّة!

غَنّى سَوّى غطّى صَلّى

ملّى/عبّى ربّى هوّى

ماضي	مُضارع	لازم +	أمِر

سَوّيت	بَسَوّي	أسَوّي	
سَوّينا	بِنْسَوّي	نْسَوّي	
سَوّيت	بِتْسَوّي	تْسَوّي	سَوّي
سَوّيتي	بِتْسَوّي	تْسَوّي	سَوّي
سَوّيتوا	بِتْسَوّوا	تْسَوّوا	سَوّوا
سَوّى	بْيسَوّي	يْسَوّي	
سَوّت	بِتسَوّي	تْسَوّي	
سَوّوا	بْيِسَوّوا	يْسَوّوا	

ما تسَوّي! ما تْسَوّي! ما تْسَوّوا!

أكتب/ي 1.بالماضي شو عملت/ي إمبارح 2. بالمُضارِع شو بتعمل كُل يوم

صِحي / قام من النوم راح على الحَمّام غَسَل وجه

حَضّر الفطور شِرِب قهوة لِبِس أواعي

طِلِع مِن البيت مِشي/ أخذ الباص/السيّارة

وِصِل على الشُّغُل كَتَب/بَعَث إيميلات حِضِر إجتماع

خَلّص شُغُل مَرَق على السوق/ الدكّان

رِجِع / طَبَخ /أكَل نَظّف / جَلى/ رَتّب

زار العيلة/ شاف الأصحاب

رَكَض/ لفّ /صلّى /قَرَأ/ أخذ دوش/

فَكّر شوي/ نسي كل شي / نام

كيف بْنعمل المَقلوبة؟؟

قَطّع/ حطّ 2/ جاب/نَظّف/ شَوى/ غَسَل/

راح/ جَرّب/نِسي/حَضّر/ قَشّر/ وَسّخ/ جلى

أوّل إشي إنتَ لازم_______ على السوق عَشان_______ الخُضرة.

_______ كُل الأغراض الضَروريّة: الرُزوالزيت والزَّهرة والجَزر والبيتنجان والبَصَل وما_______ البْهارات والمَلح.

_______ الخُضرة و_______ الجزر والبَصَل والبيتنجان.

_______ كُل الخُضْرة شُقَف صغيرة وبَعدين _______ في الفُرن.

بَعدين ________ الرُز والخُضرة مَع بعض في الطَنجرة على الغاز مع شويّة زيت. وضروري ______ بهارات المقلوبة والمَلح. وصُبّ المي فوقهُم. كُل كاسة رُز بدها كاستين مي!!!

_______ ما _______ المَطبخ ☹

ما تنسى________ الصحون و________ كُلّ شي .

صَحتين وعافية!!!!

على قَلبَك/ قَلبِك/ قلبكُم

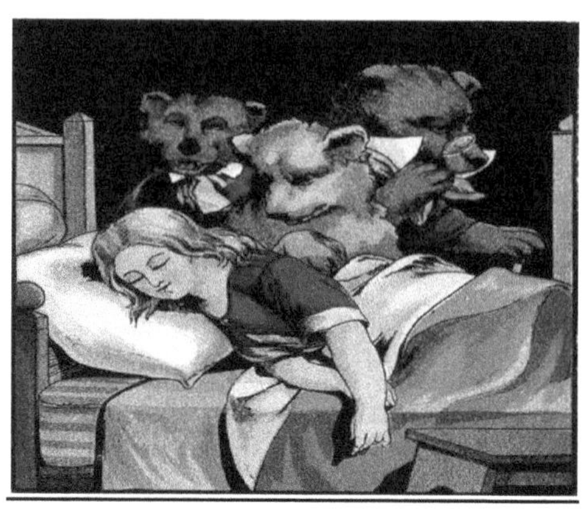

قصّة البنت إلّي شَعَرها ذَهبي

كان يا ما كان في قديم الزّمان، كان فيه بِنت ساكنة في الغابة، وكان شَعَرها كتير أشقر عَشان هيك الناس كانوا **يسَمّوها** البِنت إلّي شعرها ذَهَبي. كان بِدها تعرف شو كان فيه في الغابة و**قرّرت** تروح هناك بَس ما **خبّرَت** إمّها. الطّقس كان حلو، وهي مَشَت بين الورد ورَكضت بين الشَّجر. بَعدين لمّا حَسّت حالها تَعبانة **دوَّرت** على مكان عشان تُقعُد. وفجأةً، شافَت مِن بعيد بيت صغير و**فَكّرت** تروح هُناك و**كمّلت** طَريقها. و لمّا وصلَت، دقّت على الباب بَس ما حَدا ردّ، عشان هيك فاتت على البيت. شافت طاولة كبيرة كان عليها تلَت صحون رُزّ : كبير ووَسَط وصغير. كانَت كتير جُعانة، **فَجَرّبت** تاكُل من الصَّحِن الكبير بس كان كتير سُخُن، والوَسَط كان كتير بارِد أمّا الصغير كان مُمْتاز فَأكَلَتُه كُلُّه!!!!

و لمّا قَعْدَت كان الكُرسي الكبير كتير عالي، والوَسَط كتير يابِس، أمّا الصّغير كان مُناسِب، بَسْ للأسَف كَسْرَتُه عَشانها ثقيلة!!! ☹

بعد الأكِل، حَسَّت حالها نَعْسانة فَطِلعَت على الدّرَج ودَخْلت على غُرفة النّوم وشافت تَلَت تخوت، **جَرَّبَتْهُم** وكان التخت الكبير كتير يابِس والتخت الوسط كتير طري أمّا التَّخت الصّغير كان كتير منيح. نامت عَليه ولمّا صِحيت شافت تَلت دُبَبة حَولين التّخت، هي خافت كتير وهَرْبت وما رِجْعَت أمّا الدُببة التّلاتة ما فِهموا شو صار!!!!!

ومين كانت هالبنت!!!؟؟ بَس الدُّب الصّغير كان كتير زعلان عشان أكلت صَحْنُه وكّسْرت كُرسيه ونامت على تَختُه!!

أُكتب/ي خَمس أسئلة عَن القُصّة

ضَمير المَفعول به

- سَلمى: يا ميرا، إنتِ كُنتي إمْبارح بالسّينما، أنا ما شُفتِك؟
- ميرا: أيوا، أنا كُنت هُناك وشُفت سَمير جَنب السّينما وهو قالّي إنُّه شافِك.
- سَلمى: أنا كَمان شُفتُه عَشان هيك عْرِفت إنُّه كُنتي هُناك☺

فِعِل + ضَمير المَفْعول به

شاف(أنا)	=	شافْني
شاف(إحنا)	=	شافْنا
شاف(إنتَ)	=	شافَك
شاف(إنتِ)	=	شافِك
شاف(إنتوا)	=	شافْكُم
شاف(هو)	=	شافُه
شاف(هي)	=	شافها
شاف(هم)	=	شافهُم

– أنا كَتَبت الوَظيفة إمْبارح ← أنا كَتَبتها إمْبارح.

– الولاد بِدهم يُرسموا البحر ← الولاد بِدهُم يُرْسُموه

يُرسمو⊗ ه

_ المعلمة: يا طُلّاب مُمْكِن أمحي اللوح؟

_ الطُلّاب: أيوا، إمحيه، لَوْسَمَحتي.

إمْحي+ ـُـه = إمْحيه

– السِكريترة بَعْثت الإيميل؟ لا، لِسّا ما بَعْثَتُه.

– إنتَ جِبت الأغْراض مِن السوق؟ أيوا، جِبتهُم / ـها.

– بْتِعرَفي تُطْبُخي مَقلوبة؟ أيوا، بَعْرَف أطبُخها.

- إنتوا فْهِمْتوا السّؤال؟ لأ، إحْنا ما فْهِمناه.
- عْمِلتوا الوَظيفة؟ أيوا عملناها.
- جاوِب/ي عَن الأسئلة مع الضَمير:

1. إنتوا كَتَبْتوا الدَّرس؟ ______________________
2. الولاد ضَبّوا غُرفتهُم؟ ______________________
3. أصْحابِك بْيِبعرَفوا مَعهد پولِس؟ ______________________
4. زُرْتوا روما؟ ______________________
5. بِتْحِبّ/ي الكنافة؟ ______________________
6. طفيت/ي الضَّو لمّا طلعت/ي مِن البيت؟

____

7. بتِسْمَع/ي أخْبار يَومياً؟ ______________________
8. بِدْكُم نِشْرَب القَهْوة بَرّا؟ ______________________
9. بِتْحبّ/ي تِحضر/ي أفْلام مُخيفة؟ ______________________
10. طَلَبتوا الحساب= (الفاتورة) ______________________

لَـ + ضمير

- شو جابلك أبوكي مِن سويسرا؟
- هوجابلي شوكَلاطة ☺
- شو طَبختي صحابك إمبارح على العَشا؟
- طَبَخْتلهم مقلوبة .

السيّارة مِش إلنا!

الكتاب إلي !

إسِم + إلــي

إلْـنا

إلَـك

إلِـك

إلْـكُم

إلُـه

إلْها

إلْهُم

فِعِل + ــلي

ــِلنا

ــلَك

ــلِك

ــِلْكُم

ــلُه

ــِلْها

ــِلْهُم

جاب / عِمِل / حَكى/ قال/ طَبَخ/ كَتَب/ بَعَث ....

هو جاب لـَ (إحنا) =

هم عِمِل لـَ (إنتوا) =

أنا طَبَخ لـَ (هم) =

هو قال لـَ (أنا) =

إنتَ حكى لَـ (أنا) =

الطُلّاب كتب لـَ (المعلمة) =

السِّكرتيرة بَعَث لَـ (المُوَظّفين) =

أُكْتُب الفِعِل بالأمر وبَعدين بالماضي مع الضمير إذا لازِم:

1. الإم: ياولاد، ________ شُكراً للتيتا!

الاولاد: إحنا__________ شُكراً☺ **(قال)**

2. لينا: يا سَمير، لو سَمَحت ________ المَلِح.

سمير: أنا ________ المَلِح والفِلفِل!!! **(جاب)**

3. الولاد: بابا _________ قُصَّة!!!

الأب: الصبُح _________ قُصّة طويلة، هلّأ نَعسان!!! **(حَكى)**

/مَع/مِن/ عَن/ في/ بِـ / عَلى/ لَـ

	في	عَلى	لَـ
أنا	فيّ	عَلَيّ	إلي
إحنا	فينا	عَلينا	إلْنا
إنتَ	فيك	عَليك	إلَك
إنتِ	فيكي	عَليكي	إلِك
إنتوا	فيكُم	عَليكُم	إلَكُم
هو	فيه	عَليه	إلُه
هي	فيها	عَليها	إلها
هم	فيهُم	عَليهُم	إلهُم

كَمّل مع حَرف الجَرّ المُناسب:

1) - إنتِ زعلتي ___ ؟ (أنا)

- لأ، أنا مِش زعلانة ______. (إنتَ)

2)- المُدير سأل _____ ؟ (أنا)

-أيوا، هو سأل _____. (إنتَ)

3) سَكّرتي الباب منيح؟

أيوا سكّرتُه __ المُفتاح.

4) وين المَلِح؟

حَطّيتُه ____ الطاولة.

5) بعثتي الإيميل __ السِّكرتيرة؟

آه، بعثتُه ورَدّت _____. (أنا)

6) كيف سافَرْتوا ___ اليونان؟__ السّفينة وِلّا __ الطيّارة؟

7) فَكّرت ___ (إحنا) لَمّا كنت في فَرَنسا؟ آه، فَكّرت ____ (إنتوا) و هادي الجبنة والنبيد _____ (إنتوا) ___ هُناك.

8) ما أحلا هالفُستان _____ (إنتِ)!!!

9) لِسا بِتدَوّر ____ شُغُل؟

10) إنتَ حضِرت الدرس إمبارح؟

-لأ، أنا غِبت ____.

11) هادي الهِديّة _____ (مِن /هي)؟

أيوا، _____ ______. (مِن هي) (لَ /إنتوا).

12) أنا متأخّر _____ الدرس؟

لأ، إنتَ مش مِتأخّر ______.

13) شققة الكيك _____ ؟ (لَ/ أنا)

نعم، _____ (لَ/ إنتِ).

14) __ مين رايحة __ السينما؟

- رايحة ___ أصْحابي.

15) يا إمّي الولاد رَدّوا ____؟ (إنتِ)

- آه كانوا كتير شاطرين و ردّوا __

(أنا).

16) ضَبّيت الأواعي ____ الشّنتة؟

أيوا، ضَبّيتهُم_____.

17) هلا إبنِك بيعرف ينزل__/__ الدَرج؟

أيوا، بيعرَف يطْلَع ___ و ينزَل ___!

18) - إنتَ ساكِن قَريب ___ شُغلَك؟

لأ، للأسَف أنا ساكِن بعيد ___.

-وكيف بتروح _____ _ السيّارة وِلا __ الباص؟

أنا بَفضّل أروح ___ البسكليت!!!

19) قبل ما تحِلّ التمرين فكِّر منيح ___
السؤال!!!

20) درستوا الإمتحان ___ بَعض؟

لأ، كُل واحد درسه لحالُه.

ظروف المَكان والزمان

بَعِد/ قَبِل/ قُدّام/ وَرا / فوق / تَحِت/ جنب=جمب / عِند/ قبال/ حولين

	قُدّام	ورا	عِند
أنا	قُدّامي	وراي	عِندي
إحنا		وَرانا	
إنتَ		وَراك	
إنتِ		وَراكي	
إنتوا		وَراكُم	
هو		وَراه	
هي		وَراها	
هم		وَراهُم	

كَمّل مع ظَرف الزمان او المكان المُناسب:

1) ليش قَعدت بعيد؟ تعال ___ (أنا).

2) أنا ساكنة في الطابِق الارضي وإمّي ساكنة _____.(فوق/ أنا)

3) يا ولاد ما تلِفّوا ____ الطاولة، بِدّي أشوف التلفزيون!!!

4) عيوني بيوجعوني عشان كل يوم أنا بكون____ الشاشة لَوقت طويل!

5) لمّا بعزم شخص علي بيتي أنا بَقول : تفَضّل ______.

6) الماضي ______ (إحنا) والمستقبل ______ (إحنا)!!!

7) في الدّور: انا ____، لو سَمحت إحجزلي مَكاني، هَلّأ بَرجع !!

8) لَمّا بَرَتّب البيت دايماً الألعاب والطابات بيكونوا ____ التخت!!!

9) كُل يوم بقول صباح الخير للجيران إلي ساكنين ______ . (قبال/أنا)

10) في السيّارة الولاد الصغار لازم يُقعدوا____ والكبار ______.

11) يا ولاد أُغسُلوا إيديكُم ___ الأكل و ____!!!

مِن وين إنتَ/ إنتِ؟

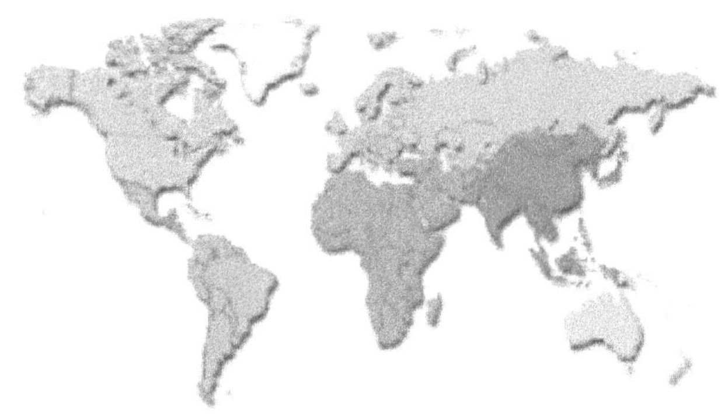

خارِطة العالم

ميرا : أنا مِن مَدينة صغيرة بَس مُهمّة كتير. مَدينتي في الشَّرق الأوسط، والنّاس فيها بيحكوا عَرَبي وعِبري بَس كَمان فيه كتير أجانِب بيزوروها. المُسلمين والمسيحيّين واليَهود من كُلّ العالم بيحبّوا يجوا عَليها ويصلّوا فيها.

بتعرفوا عن أي مَدينة بَحْكي ؟

روبيرتا: ما أزْكى البيتزا هون، و ما أحلى الآثار القديمة، مَدينتي عاصمة إيطاليا، بتعرفوا شو هي؟

پول: أنا ساكِن في پاريس ومِن بيتي بَقدر أشوف نهر السّين، و إنتَ وين ساكِن؟

جون: أنا ساكِن في قَرية حِلوة جَنوب فَرنسا.

مْعَلمة الجُغرافية : يا طُلّاب، اليوم راح نُدْرس عن قارّة أفريقيا.

طالِب تونِسي: أنا مِن تونِس بَلَدي مَوْجود في <u>شَمال</u> أفريقيا.

و إنتَ/تِ مِن وين؟ مِن مَدينة ولّا قَرية؟ في أي قارّة بَلَدك؟

مُفْرَد		جَمع
شارِع	-	شوارِع
حارة	-	حارات
بَلْدة	-	بَلْدات
مَدينة	-	مُدُن
قَرْية	-	قُرى
بَلَد	-	بلاد/بُلدان
دَوْلة	-	دُوَل
عاصْمة	-	عَواصِم
قارّة	-	قارّات
نَهر	-	أنهار

(بَلَد = دَوْلة)

بُحَيْرة - بُحَيْرات

بَحَر - بحار

مُحيط - مُحيطات

جَبَل - جبال

مَنطِقة - مَناطِق

جزيرة - جُزُر

كَمّل زي المِثال:

جِنسية - جِنسيّات جواز سَفَر

مِن فَرنسا ⟵ هو فَرَنسي/ هي فرنسيّة

مِن مَصِر ⟵ هو ______/ هي ______

مِن النّمسا ⟵ هو ______/ هي ______

مِن الصّين ⟵ هو ______/ هي ______

إعلان/ دِعاية

1.يَلّا____ عَلى أحْلى جَزيرِة في اليونان،2. ____البَحر الأزْرَق3 . و____في أحْسن المَطاعِم 4. و _____السَّلطة اليونانيّة وأزكى سَمَك في العالم! ما5 . ____مَرتين!!!

ما6. ____،عِنّا أحْسَن الأسْعار!!7. ____العْيلة و8.____ أحلى عُطْلة! و لمّا تِرجع 9._____ أصحابَك !!!

سانتوريني، ما أحْلى الطَّقس هُناك!

إنتَ لسّا في البيت ؟؟؟ 10._____و11._____ رِحلة من العُمر!!!

خاف	قام	عاش	داق
حَجَز	أكَل	فكّر	جاب
		خَبّر	شاف
		أجى	

يعطيكُم ألف عافية
بشوفكم في مُستوى أربعة ☺☺☺

www.ingramcontent.com/pod-product-compliance
Ingram Content Group UK Ltd.
Pitfield, Milton Keynes, MK11 3LW, UK
UKHW061829190726
13853UKWH00009B/2513